Teen Addictions & Recovery Workbook

Facilitator Reproducible Self-Assessments, Exercises & Educational Handouts

John J. Liptak, EdD
Ester A. Leutenberg

Illustrated by
Amy L. Brodsky, LISW-S

wholeperson
Stress & Wellness Publishers
Duluth, Minnesota

Whole Person
101 W. 2nd St., Suite 203
Duluth, MN 55802

800-247-6789

books@wholeperson.com
www.wholeperson.com

Teen Addictions & Recovery Workbook
Facilitator Reproducible Self-Assessments,
Exercises & Educational Handouts

Copyright ©2013 by John J. Liptak and Ester A. Leutenberg.
All rights reserved. Except for short excerpts for review purposes and materials in the assessment, journaling activities, and educational handouts sections, no part of this book may be reproduced or transmitted in any form by any means, electronic or mechanical without permission in writing from the publisher. Self-assessments, exercises, and educational handouts are meant to be photocopied.

All efforts have been made to ensure accuracy of the information contained in this book as of the date published. The author(s) and the publisher expressly disclaim responsibility for any adverse effects arising from the use or application of the information contained herein.

Printed in the United States of America

10 9 8 7 6 5 4 3 2 1

Editorial Director: Carlene Sippola
Art Director: Joy Morgan Dey

Library of Congress Control Number: 2013936468
ISBN: 978-1-57025-300-3

For the Professional Using This Book

Addiction is the continued use of a mind or mood-altering substance, compulsive thoughts and behavior, or engagement in a compulsive activity that despite its negative consequences is continued by the user. It usually begins with a person over-doing a habit.

Classic hallmarks of addiction include impaired control over substances or behavior, preoccupation with substance or behavior, continued use despite consequences, and denial. Habits and patterns associated with addiction are typically characterized by immediate gratification (short-term rewards), coupled with delayed deleterious effects (long-term costs).

The word addiction conjures up someone who abuses drugs or alcohol. However, any substance, activity, or behavior can be considered an addiction if it becomes the major focus of a person's life to the exclusion of other activities, or that it begins to harm the person's psychological, social, mental, or emotional well-being. For example:

- **Substance-Related:** In this type of addiction, the person uses mind and mood-altering substances such as alcohol, speed and prescription drugs.
- **Compulsive Activities:** In this type of addiction, the person compulsively engages in such activities as shopping, gambling, exercising, or use of computers.
- **Compulsive Behaviors:** In this type of addiction, the person compulsively engages in behaviors that become self-destructive in such activities as sex and eating disorders.

Many people often confuse addictions and habits. Habits and addictions often seem like the same thing, but they are very different. Habits are developed by choice, whereas addictions grow because people are often unable to control the aspects of their cravings. They cannot control how much to consume or engage in and become dependent on it to cope with everyday life. Addictions, unlike habits, meet a psychological or physical need of the person addicted, and because of this, the person has a difficult time stopping.

Some common characteristics of addictions:

- Person becomes obsessed with the activity, substance, or behavior and cannot stop thinking about it.
- Compulsive attention to the addiction usually causes the person harm (i.e., problems in school, with friends and family, and with people in the community).
- Person will engage in the activity over and over even though the person wants to stop.
- Regardless if it is a psychological addiction (shopping) or a physical addiction (alcohol or heroine), withdrawing from the addiction causes withdrawal symptoms (shaking, cold sweats, cravings).
- The person often loses control of when, how often, and how much he or she engages in the activity.
- The person often denies having the addiction.

You will need to use your clinical judgment in determining whether the assessments and activities will be effective for the population with whom you work. There may be some handouts you will not use because they do not fit the needs of your population. If your clients are working on other programs, you will want to make sure that the exercises and journaling activities do not conflict with the program's objectives. On the next page is a list of possible addictions. As you come across others, you may wish to add them to that list.

(Continued on the next page)

For the Professional Using This Book *(continued)*
Possible Teen Habits and/or Addictions

- Alcohol
- Arson
- Betting
- Body building
- Bullying, sadism, masochism
- Caffeine
- Carbohydrates
- Card playing
- Collecting objects
- Computer games
- Crime
- Cyber sex
- Diuretics
- Eating disorders
- Email
- Food
- Exercise
- Fanaticizing excessively
- Gambling
- Illicit drugs
- Internet
- Legal drugs
- Love obsessively
- Marijuana
- Money
- Nicotine
- Online games
- Over-the-counter medications
- Pornography
- Prescription drugs
- Relationship attention and neediness
- Risky behavior
- Self-injury
- Sex
- Sexting
- Shopping
- Shopping online
- Smoking
- Sleeping too much or not enough
- Social networking sites
- Solvents
- Spending money
- Sports
- Stealing/Shop-lifting
- Steroids
- Sugar
- Texting
- Thrill-seeking
- Tranquilizers
- Video games
- Work

(Continued on the next page)

For the Professional Using This Book *(continued)*

The *Teen Addictions & Recovery Workbook* contains six separate sections to help participants learn more about themselves as well how addictions are impacting their lives.

- **Do I Overdo My Habits? Scale** helps individuals explore those types of habits they tend to overdo and identify ways to overcome these negative habits.
- **Am I Likely to be Addicted? Scale** helps individuals examine if they have a constellation of personality traits that predispose them to various addictions.
- **Am I Addicted? Scale** helps individuals to determine the level of their addiction to substances, activities and/or thought and behaviors.
- **Am I Relapsing? Scale** helps individuals identify the changes in thinking, feeling and behavior that accompany relapse.
- **Can I Stop? Scale** helps individuals define a clearer picture of the excuses that they may be using to continue their addiction and guides them to ways they can stop.
- **Change and Recovery Scale** helps individuals explore the level of self-discipline and will power they have in combatting addictions.

These sections serve as an avenue for individual self-reflection, as well as group experiences revolving around identified topics of importance. Each assessment includes directions for easy administration, scoring and interpretation. Value of these self assessments:

- They take into account life experiences of different clients.
- They take into account similarities across cultures and unique aspects of cultures that may possibly be influencing members of the culture.
- They recognize but do not pathologize people from different cultures.
- They respect *norms* established for populations similar to those with whom you are working.
- They serve as non-threatening measures.

Each section includes exploratory activities, reflective journaling exercises and educational handouts to help participants to discover their habitual and ineffective methods of managing substance abuse, and to explore new ways for bringing about healing.

In the past twenty years, many research studies have focused on the value of self-reflection and journaling as a way of exploring personal characteristics, identifying ineffective behaviors and examining thoughts and feelings that lead to ineffective behaviors. This book is unique with its combination of two powerful psychological tools for substance abuse and recovery management: self-assessment and journaling.

The art of self-reflection goes back many centuries and is rooted in many of the world's greatest spiritual and philosophical traditions. Socrates, the ancient Greek philosopher, was known to walk the streets engaging the people he met in philosophical reflection and dialogue. He felt that this type of activity was so important in life that he proclaimed, "The unexamined life is not worth living!" The unexamined life is one in which the same routine is continually repeated without ever thinking about its meaning to one's life and how this life really could be lived. However, a *structured* reflection and examination of beliefs, assumptions, characteristics and patterns can provide a better understanding which can lead to a more satisfying personal life and career. A greater level of self-understanding about important life skills is often necessary to make positive, self-directed changes in the negative patterns that keep repeating throughout life. The assessments and exercises in this book can help promote this self-understanding. Through involvement in the in-depth activities, the participant claims ownership in the development of positive patterns.

By combining reflective assessment and journaling, your participants will engage in methods to reduce and discontinue their addictions.

The Assessments, Journaling Activities & Educational Handouts

The Assessments, Journaling Activities, and Educational Handouts in this book are reproducible and ready to be photocopied for participants' use. Assessments contained in this book have been developed and designed just like any other test, inventory or assessment on the market. They are similar to the ones used by psychologists, counselors and career consultants. Inventories and interpretations are based on self-reported data. In other words, the accuracy and usefulness of the information provided is dependent on the honest and truthful information that participants provide about themselves. Participants may not learn much from taking some of the inventories, or they might verify some information that they already know. On the other hand, they may uncover information that might be keeping them from being as happy or as successful as they might be. Either way, the important thing is that they are honest about themselves.

An assessment instrument can provide the participants with valuable information about themselves; however, it cannot measure or identify everything. Its purpose is not to pigeon-hole certain characteristics, but rather to allow participants to explore all of their characteristics. This book contains informal assessments and not *traditional tests*. Tests measure knowledge or whether something is right or wrong. For the assessments in this book, there are no right or wrong answers. These assessments ask for only opinions or attitudes about a topic of importance in the participant's career and life.

When administering the assessments in this book to your clients or students, remember that unlike traditional assessment inventories, the items are generically written so that they will be applicable to a wide variety of people; therefore, they will not account for every possible variable for every person. No assessment is specifically tailored to one person, so people completing the assessments must be flexible in their approach to completing, scoring and interpreting the responses. Thus, participants should not spend too much time trying to analyze the content of the questions on the assessments; rather, they should simply think about questions in general and then spontaneously report how they feel about each statement.

The results participants find from taking the assessments and completing the journaling exercises will also vary from person to person. Some people will experience insights that might change their lives and how they approach living. For others, however, results may not be as dramatic. For some, taking the assessments might bring new information from their unconscious to consciousness where problems can be worked on. Other people may simply learn things about themselves that they never knew, or they may receive confirmation about positive aspects in their lives. Whatever the results of an assessment, encourage participants to talk about their findings and their feelings about what they discovered about themselves.

Use Codes for Confidentiality

Confidentiality is a term for any action that preserves the privacy of other people. Because teens completing the activities in this workbook might be asked to answer assessment items and to journal about and explore their relationships, you will need to discuss confidentiality between their peers before you begin using the materials in this workbook. Maintaining confidentiality between their peers is important as it shows respect for others and allows participants to explore their feelings without hurting anyone's feelings or fearing gossip, harm or retribution.

In a school group situation, explain to the participants that they need to assign a name code for each person they write about as they complete the various activities in the workbook. For example, a friend named Joey who enjoys going to hockey games might be titled JLHG (Joey Loves Hockey Games) for a particular exercise. In order to protect their friends' identities, they should not use people's actual names or initials, just codes.

It is your duty to warn a trusted adult if a participant is being harmed or is harming another person, or has intentions of killing him/herself or another person.

Layout of the Book

The *Teen Addictions & Recovery Workbook* is designed to be used either independently or as part of an integrated curriculum. You may administer one of the assessments and the journaling exercises to an individual or a group with whom you are working, or you may administer a number of the assessments over one or more days.

This Book Includes:

- **Assessment Instruments** – Self-assessment inventories with scoring directions and interpretation materials. Group facilitators can choose one or more of the activities relevant to their participants.
- **Activity Handouts** – Practical questions and activities that prompt self-reflection and promote self-understanding. These questions and activities foster introspection and promote pro-social behaviors.
- **Reflective Questions for Journaling** – Self-exploration activities and journaling exercises specific to each assessment to enhance self-discovery, learning and healing.
- **Educational Handouts** – Handouts designed to enhance instruction can be used individually or in groups to promote a positive understanding of addictions and to provide positive reinforcement for recovery. The handouts can be distributed, converted into masters for overheads or transparencies, or written on a board and discussed.

Who Should Use This Program?
This book has been designed as a practical tool for helping professionals, such as therapists, counselors, psychologists, doctors, teachers and group leaders. Depending on the role of the professional using The *Teen Addictions & Recovery Workbook* and the specific group's needs, these sections can be used individually or combined for a more comprehensive approach.

Why Use Self-Assessments?
Self-assessments are important in teaching various addiction management skills because they help participants to . . .

- Become aware of the primary motivators that guide their behavior.
- Explore and learn to *let go* of troublesome habits and behavioral patterns learned in childhood.
- Explore the effects of unconscious childhood messages.
- Gain insight and focus on behavioral change.
- Uncover inner-resources that can help them to cope better with problems and difficulties.
- Explore personal characteristics without judgment.
- Be fully aware of personal strengths and weaknesses.

Because the assessments are presented in a straightforward and easy-to-use format, individuals can self-administer, score, and interpret each assessment at their own pace.

Thanks to the following whose input in this book has been extraordinary!

Amy Brodsky, LISW-S
Annette Damien, MS, PPS
Deborah Fernandez-Turner, DO, FAPA
Beth Jennings, CTEC Counselor
Hannah Lavoie, Teenager

Jay Leutenberg, Pr.E.
Kathy Liptak, EdD
Eileen Regen, M.Ed., CJE
Laurie A. Rathman, M.Ed., CAGS
Margie Williams, MC, LISAC, LPC

Amy Hirshberg Lederman, J.D., M.J.EdD

Introduction for the Teen Participant

An addiction refers to an over-indulgence in, and a physical and/or emotional dependence on, a variety of substances, activities, thoughts and/or behaviors. Teen addictions come in many different shapes and forms. When most people hear the word addiction, they usually think of drug use and abuse. In reality, many different types of addictive behaviors exist. Addictions have very different effects on the body and mind of the person. Different types of addictions include drugs and alcohol, caffeine, cigarettes, steroids, computer use and social networking, gambling, tobacco, video games, texting, pornography, sex, sugar, money, shopping, self-injury, exercising, thrill-seeking and prescription drugs.

Teens have these addictions for a variety of complicated reasons including:

- To fit in
- To be accepted
- To change an image
- To feel more social
- To get in with a specific clique of peers
- To feel excited when bored
- To distance themselves from family
- To provide distance from school problems
- To relax from pressures of everyday life
- To gain confidence and loosen inhibitions
- To boost self-esteem
- To feel less lonely
- To "numb" feelings
- To feel important
- To feel less depressed
- To feel less anxious
- To rebel
- To seem "cool"

An addiction is a disease that negatively affects emotions, thinking and behavior. Once a person begins the path to an addiction, the effects on that person's brain and body will make him/her want to continue. That person will know that he/she has an addiction problem when continuing to do it even though it causes problems in relationships at home or at school, with money, with the law, or with health. Addictions usually cause one to engage in that activity more and more to stay satisfied. Often what is perceived as positive effects are actually negative in the long run.

The good news is that if you feel as if you possibly have a habit that is becoming a problem, the activities included in this book can help you commit to a plan to ensure that you can break this habit.

CONFIDENTIALITY

You will be asked to respond to assessments and exercises and to journal about some experiences in your life. Everyone has the right to confidentiality, and you need to honor the right of their privacy. Think about it this way – you would not want someone writing things about you that other people could read. Your friends feel this way also.

In order to maintain the confidentiality of your friends, assign people code names based on things you know about them. For example, a friend named Sherry who loves to wear purple might be coded as SWP (Sherry Wears Purple). **Do not use any person's actual name when you are listing people – only name codes.**

Teen Addiction & Recovery Workbook
TABLE OF CONTENTS

SECTION I – Do I Overdo My Habits? Scale

Do I Overdo My Habits? Scale Directions 15
Do I Overdo My Habits? Substances Scale 16
Do I Overdo My Habits? Excessive Activities Scale 17
Do I Overdo My Habits? Obsessive Thoughts
    and Behaviors Scale 18
Scoring Directions 19
Profile Interpretation 19

Exercises

About My Substances 20
About My Excessive Activities 21
About My Thoughts and Behaviors 22

SECTION II – Am I Likely to be Addicted? Scale

Am I Likely to be Addicted? Scale Directions 25
Am I Likely to be Addicted? Scale 26–27
Scoring Directions 28
Profile Interpretation 29
Scale Descriptions 30

Exercises

What Boosts My Self-Esteem? My School or
    Work/Volunteer Accomplishments. 31
What Boosts My Self-Esteem?
    My Family or Recreation/Sports Accomplishments 32
Family Relationships 33
Friend Relationships3 34
Life Skills 35
Distractions 36
My Risky Distractions 37
"Socially Acceptable" 38

SECTION III – Am I Addicted? Scale

Habits I Overdo (For Your Eyes Only) 40
Am I Addicted? Scale Directions. 41
Am I Addicted? Scale 42–43
Scoring Directions 44
Profile Interpretation 45
Scale Descriptions 46

TABLE OF CONTENTS (Continued)

Exercises
  Problems in My Life 47–49
  Self-Defeating Behaviors 50
  Triggers 51
  Growing Up with Addiction around Me 52
  What about Me? 53
  Non-Addicted People 54–56
  Peer Pressure 57
  Feeling Scared 58
  Denial that Addiction Exists 59

SECTION IV – Am I Relapsing? Scale
  Am I Relapsing? Scale Directions 63
  Am I Relapsing? Scale 64–66
  Scoring Directions 67
  Profile Interpretation 67
  Scale Descriptions 68

Exercises
  Changes in your Thinking 69
  Changes in your Feelings 70
  Changes in your Behavior 71
  My History 72–73
  Recovery Management 74–75
  How Thinking Affects Potential Relapse 76
  How Feelings Affect Potential Relapse 77
  How Behavior Affects Potential Relapse 78
  Plan for Action to Prevent Relapse 79
  Relapse Quotations 80

SECTION V – Can I Stop? Scale
  Can I Stop? Scale Directions 83
  Can I Stop? Scale 84–85
  Scoring Directions 86
  Profile Interpretation 86

Exercises
  Mental Roadblocks 87–88
  Permission-Giving Thoughts for Mental Roadblocks 89
  Financial Roadblocks 90–91
  Emotional Roadblocks 92
  Physical Roadblocks 93–95
  I Can Stop! 96
  Peer Pressure 97

Educational Handout
  Stages of Addiction 98

TABLE OF CONTENTS (Continued)

SECTION VI – Change & Recovery Scale
Change & Recovery Scale Directions 101
Change & Recovery Scale. 102
Scoring Directions 103
Profile Interpretation 103

Exercise
Overcoming Addictions – Goals for Change 104
Self-Worth and Self-Esteem. 105–106
Life is Very Interesting 107–109
Alternatives to Your Addictions 110
Benefits of Recovery Exercise 111
Benefits of Recovery Examples 112

Quotations
Quotation: Change. 113
Quotation: Work in Progress 114
Quotation: Control. 115
Quotation: Feeling Feelings 116
Quotation: Understanding Addictions 117
Quotation: Consequences 118
Quotation: A Wish 119

Journaling Activity
Serenity Prayer. 120

SECTION I:

Do I Overdo My Habits? Scale

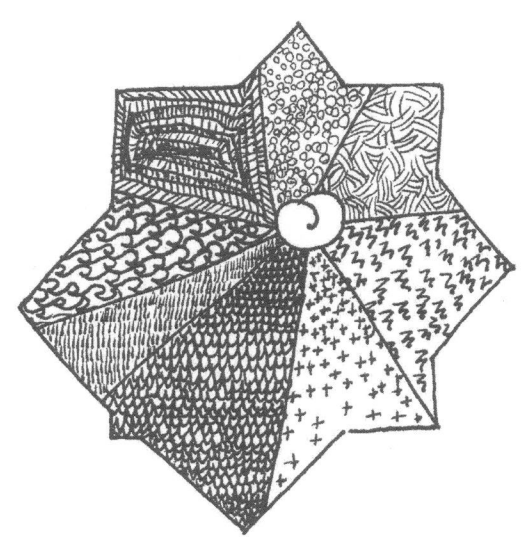

Name_____

Date_____

SECTION I: DO I OVERDO MY HABITS? SCALE

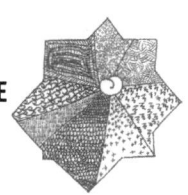

Do I Overdo My Habits?
Scale Directions

A habit is an acquired pattern regularly followed until it becomes almost involuntary. Nobody sets out to intentionally overdo a habit, but repeated use of substances, engaging excessively in activities, or having obsessive thoughts and behaviors, can lead to a problem almost without our knowing it. People can become reliant on their habits, regardless of how negatively they affect physical, mental, social and emotional consequences. They can become addicted. An addiction goes beyond how the person participates in the habit and can cross over to being extremely difficult to quit due to psychological, emotional, habitual and physical withdrawal symptoms.

On the three pages that follow, place a check mark ☑ for the habits that you may be overdoing, becoming reliant on or struggling with. For this particular scale, it is considered overdoing when you recognize that some or all of these are true for you.

- ❑ You become obsessed with the activity, substance or behavior, and cannot stop thinking about it.
- ❑ The attention you pay to the habit usually causes you harm (i.e., problems in school, with friends and family, with legal consequences, and with people in the community).
- ❑ You engage in the activity over and over, even though you want to stop.
- ❑ When you do not engage in the addiction, you feel withdrawal symptoms.
- ❑ You often deny overdoing this habit.
- ❑ You spend a lot of time and money on this habit.

This is not a test, and there are no right or wrong answers. Do not spend too much time thinking about your answers. Your initial response will likely be the most true for you. Be sure to respond to every statement. **Be honest! No one else needs to see these pages.**

(Turn to the next page and begin)

SECTION I: DO I OVERDO MY HABITS? SCALE

Do I Overdo My Habits? Substances Scale

- ❏ Alcohol (wine, beer, liquor, whiskey)
- ❏ Caffeine (energy drinks, coffee, tea, soft drinks, chocolate)
- ❏ Carbohydrates
- ❏ Cocaine
- ❏ Diuretics
- ❏ Food
- ❏ Illicit drugs
- ❏ Legal drugs
- ❏ Marijuana
- ❏ Over-the-Counter Medications
- ❏ Nicotine (cigarettes, cigars, chewing tobacco)
- ❏ Prescription drugs
- ❏ Smoking
- ❏ Solvents (glue, aerosol sprays, gasoline)
- ❏ Steroids
- ❏ Sugar
- ❏ Tranquilizers
- ❏ _____
- ❏ _____
- ❏ _____

TOTAL = _____

(Continued on the next page)

SECTION I: DO I OVERDO MY HABITS? SCALE

Do I Overdo My Habits? Excessive Activities Scale

- ❑ Body building
- ❑ Card playing
- ❑ Collecting objects
- ❑ Email
- ❑ Exercise
- ❑ Gambling
- ❑ Internet
- ❑ Online games
- ❑ Sex
- ❑ Shopping
- ❑ Shopping online
- ❑ Social networking sights
- ❑ Sports
- ❑ Texting
- ❑ Thrills
- ❑ Video games
- ❑ Work
- ❑ _____
- ❑ _____
- ❑ _____

TOTAL = _____

(Continued on the next page)

SECTION I: DO I OVERDO MY HABITS? SCALE

Do I Overdo My Habits?
Obsessive Thoughts and Behaviors Scale

- ❑ Arson
- ❑ Betting
- ❑ Bullying, sadism, masochism
- ❑ Crime
- ❑ Cyber sex
- ❑ Eating disorders (calorie counting, food restricting, purging, over-eating)
- ❑ Fanaticizing excessively
- ❑ Obsessive love
- ❑ Over-sleeping
- ❑ Procrastination
- ❑ Relationship neediness
- ❑ Risky behavior (driving when using or texting)
- ❑ Self-injury (cutting, burning, hair-pulling)
- ❑ Sexting
- ❑ Spending money
- ❑ Stealing/shop-lifting
- ❑ Watching or reading pornography
- ❑ _____
- ❑ _____
- ❑ _____

TOTAL = _____

(Go to the Scoring Directions on the next page)

SECTION I: DO I OVERDO MY HABITS? SCALE

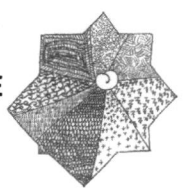

Do I Overdo My Habits?
Scoring

The *Do I Overdo My Habits?* scale is designed to help you explore the various types of habits you may be overdoing in three categories: Substances, Excessive Activities, and Thoughts and Behaviors.

To score this scale:

For each of the sections, count the number of boxes in which you placed a ✓. Include the blank lines. You will receive a score from 0 to 20. Put that total on the line marked TOTAL at the end of each section.

Then, transfer your totals for each of the three sections to the corresponding lines below:

Do I Overdo My Habits? Substances   Total _____

Do I Overdo My Habits? Excessive Activities   Total _____

Do I Overdo My Habits? Thoughts and Behaviors   Total _____

Profile Interpretation

Many habits when overdone can turn into addictions and can be dangerous and unhealthy, and they can cause serious problems. Some people will just have one while others may have multiple.

Whether you have one or several, you will benefit from the exercises that follow.

Complete a separate page (pages 20, 21, 22) for each of the substances, excessive activities and thoughts and behaviors that you listed.

SECTION I: ACTIVITY HANDOUTS

About My Substances

**Referring to the items you checked off on the scale,
write one of the substances you overdo.**

_____

When did you start using this substance?

_____
_____
_____

What or who prompted you to begin using this substance? (use name codes)

_____
_____
_____

How does using this substance benefit or help you?

_____
_____
_____

In what ways is this substance causing problems for you?

_____
_____
_____

What is the negative impact of the substance in your life?

_____
_____
_____

How do you manage this substance?

_____
_____
_____

SECTION I: ACTIVITY HANDOUTS

About My Excessive Activities

**Referring to the items you checked off on the scale,
write one of the activities you overdo.**

_____

When did you start this excessive activity?
_____
_____
_____

What or who prompted you to begin this activity? (use name codes)
_____
_____
_____

How does this activity benefit or help you?
_____
_____
_____

In what ways does this activity cause problems for you?
_____
_____
_____

What is the negative impact of this activity in your life?
_____
_____
_____

How do you manage this activity?
_____
_____
_____

SECTION I: ACTIVITY HANDOUTS

About My Thoughts and Behaviors

Referring to the items you checked off on the scale, write one of the thoughts or behaviors you overdo.

_____

When did you start this thought or behavior?
_____
_____
_____

What or who prompted you to begin this thought or behavior? (use name codes)
_____
_____
_____

How does this thought or behavior benefit or help you?
_____
_____
_____

In what ways is this thought or behavior causing problems for you?
_____
_____
_____

What is the negative impact of this thought or behavior in your life?
_____
_____
_____

How do you manage this thought or behavior?
_____
_____
_____

SECTION II:

Am I Likely to be Addicted? Scale

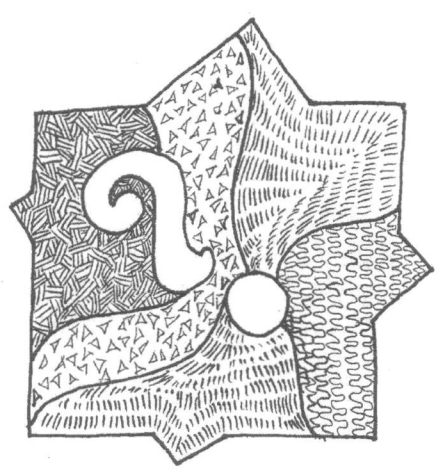

Name_____

Date_____

SECTION II: AM I LIKELY TO BE ADDICTED? SCALE

Am I Likely to be Addicted? Scale Directions

An addiction is often defined as an abnormal relationship with a substance like tobacco or alcohol, an activity like watching television or surfing the Internet, or a thought like procrastination or a behavior like gambling. An addiction often begins as a pleasurable activity in which you voluntarily participate, but it ends in compulsion, a loss of control of your actions, and the need to repeat the action even though it may be harmful to you. The *Am I Likely to be Addicted?* scale was designed to help you examine if you have a cluster of personality traits that make you vulnerable to various addictions.

This assessment contains 40 statements related to your personality. Read each of the statements and decide whether or not the statement describes you. If the statement is TRUE, circle the number next to that item under the TRUE column. If the statement is FALSE, circle the number next to that item under the FALSE column.

Pay no attention to the numbers, just the TRUE and FALSE words.

In the following example, the circled number under FALSE indicates the statement is not true of the person completing the inventory.

	TRUE	**FALSE**
People don't understand me	1	(2)

This is not a test, and there are no right or wrong answers. Do not spend too much time thinking about your answers. Your initial response will likely be the most true for you. Be sure to respond to every statement.

(Turn to the next page and begin)

SECTION II: AM I LIKELY TO BE ADDICTED? SCALE

Am I Likely to be Addicted? Scale

	TRUE	FALSE
People don't understand me	1	2
I've been called names	1	2
I feel helpless and mistreated	1	2
I don't get upset when others criticize me	2	1
I don't need the approval of others	2	1
I try to please others most of the time	1	2
I often feel inferior to my friends	1	2
I don't have a lot of freedom	1	2
I have always felt less important than others	1	2
I'm really not a good person	1	2

A. TOTAL _____

	TRUE	FALSE
I often feel isolated from other people	1	2
I often do what my friends want me to do, whether I want to or not	1	2
I am good at developing trusting relationships	2	1
I communicate well with most other people	2	1
I have trouble getting through to other people	1	2
I have trouble asking others for help	1	2
I rarely give in to pressure from my friends	2	1
I have trouble getting close to other people	1	2
It is difficult for me to develop friendships	1	2
I enjoy my friendships with others	2	1

B. TOTAL _____

(Continued on the next page)

SECTION II: AM I LIKELY TO BE ADDICTED? SCALE

Am I Likely to be Addicted? Scale *(Continued)*

	TRUE	FALSE
I often feel overwhelmed by my problems	1	2
I solve problems easily	2	1
I have trouble setting realistic goals	1	2
I usually will do anything to avoid fights	1	2
I have trouble following through on tasks	1	2
I handle stress pretty well	2	1
I rarely ignore or run away from my problems	2	1
I find myself jumping from interest to interest	1	2
I frustrate easily	1	2
I don't plan every moment of my life	2	1

C. TOTAL _____

I get bored easily	1	2
I don't want to think about my life	1	2
I have a sad life and can't do anything about it	1	2
I have many sad memories I would like to forget	1	2
I search for something to distract me from my problems	1	2
I am trying to deal with my problems	2	1
I need to find something to keep my mind occupied	1	2
I usually feel a sense of belonging	2	1
I have no meaning in my life	1	2
I am bored with my usual activities	1	2

D. TOTAL _____

(Go to the Scoring Directions on the next page)

SECTION II: AM I LIKELY TO BE ADDICTED? SCALE

Am I Likely to be Addicted? Scale
Scoring Directions

The *Am I Likely to be Addicted?* scale is designed to measure whether or not you possess an addictive personality. To get your Self-Esteem score, total the numbers that you circled for the statements marked (A) in the previous section. You will get a number from 10 to 20.
Put that number in the space marked (A) - SELF-ESTEEM TOTAL below. Then do the same for the other three scales – (B) Relationships, (C) Life Skills and (D) Distraction.

(A) – SELF-ESTEEM TOTAL = _____

(B) – RELATIONSHIPS TOTAL = _____

(C) – LIFE SKILLS TOTAL = _____

(D) – DISTRACTION TOTAL = _____

To get your overall addictive personality score, add the four scores above. Your overall score will range from 40 to 80. Put your total score in the space below:

ADDICTIVE PERSONALITY TOTAL = _____

(Go to the next page to interpret your scores)

Am I Likely to be Addicted? Scale
Profile Interpretation

Total Individual Scores	Total Score for All Four Scales	Result	Indications
17 to 20	67 to 80	high	You do not show many of the tendencies of people with addictive personalities. A high score suggests that you tend to have high self-esteem, easily develop relationships with other people, have effective life skills and engage in satisfying leisure activities but do not constantly seek leisure activities that distract you from your everyday life.
14 to 16	54 to 66	moderate	You have a moderate addictive personality, one in which you have some tendencies to have an addictive personality, but not all of the time.
10 to 13	40 to 53	low	You show many of the tendencies of people with addictive personalities. A low score suggests that you tend to have low self-esteem, often have difficulty developing effective relationships with other people, may lack appropriate life skills and often engage in leisure activities to distract you from your everyday life.

For scales which you scored in the **Moderate** or **High** range, find the descriptions on the pages that follow. Then, read the description and complete the exercises that are included. No matter how you scored, low, moderate or high, you will benefit from these exercises.

Am I Likely to be Addicted? Scale Descriptions

A – SELF-ESTEEM

People scoring low on the *Self-Esteem* section have difficulty understanding the purpose of their lives. You might wonder why you need to get up in the morning. Because of your lack of self-esteem, you start to pull away from others and pull inside of yourself. You begin to feel a general lack of self-esteem, self-control and self-confidence. As you withdraw from other people, you slowly begin to become more attached to the object of your addiction.

B – RELATIONSHIPS

People scoring low on the *Relationships* section have experienced negative relationships in life. You may have trouble trusting other people, possibly have some unhappy memories and have a difficult time creating bonds with other people. You tend not to get too close to other people or develop intimate relationships. Perhaps you are currently trying to fill an empty void that you feel because of a lack of closeness in your relationships. You may feel that your addictions offer you the promise of filling the empty void you currently feel.

C – LIFE SKILLS

People scoring low on the *Life Skills* section often lack the appropriate life skills needed to deal effectively with their predisposition to addictions. Because you have abandoned the socially acceptable ways of having your emotional needs met, you may have difficulty solving problems, communicating with others and dealing with stress in your life. You probably do not set achievable goals for yourself and are uncertain about your future. Important life skills you need to learn include ways to more effectively connect with others, develop a social support system, and identify interests that lead to greater self-esteem and self-actualization.

D – DISTRACTIONS

People scoring low on the *Distraction* section often have lives that are problematic and they feel troublesome or sad. These problems might be real or they might be perceived; they might be solvable or unsolvable. These people feel a need to be distracted from their everyday life. Instead of trying to face their problems, they want to forget them and put their minds in other places. They want to be where they do not need to think about their problems.

Regardless of your score on the *Am I Likely to be Addicted?* scale, the following exercises have been designed to help you learn more about your personality and your predisposition to the addictive personality type. The exercises that follow are designed to help you to capitalize on your strengths and overcome your weaknesses.

SECTION II: ACTIVITY HANDOUTS

What Boosts My Self-Esteem?
My School or Work/Volunteer Accomplishments

One way to start to overcome negative thoughts about yourself is to begin to look at the good things you've accomplished, not matter how small they may seem. Begin by writing your accomplishments. These do not need to be huge, just things you feel good about and that could be a source of pride for you.

Write about the school or work/volunteer activities of which you are most proud.

Things I Have Accomplished	Why It Felt Good	How it Can affect my Future
Ex: I passed my math test.	I am terrible at math. This time I really studied a lot.	I proved to myself that if I really want to do something, I can.

How can you do more of these activities?_____

_____

_____

© 2013 WHOLE PERSON ASSOCIATES, 101 W. 2ND ST., SUITE 203, DULUTH MN 55802 ▪ 800-247-6789

SECTION II: ACTIVITY HANDOUTS

What Boosts My Self-Esteem?
My Family or Recreation/Sports Accomplishments

Another way to begin to overcome an addictive personality is to take part in activities in which you feel success, rather than those which you support your addiction. Begin by writing your accomplishments. These do not need to be huge, just things you feel good about that could be a source of pride for you.

Write about the family or recreation/sports activities of which you are most proud.

Things I Have Accomplished	Why It Felt Good	How it Can affect my Future
Ex: I learned to swim	I almost drowned as a child and I decided to take lessons this summer.	I realized that I can overcome an unhappy situation in my childhood.

How can you do more of these activities?_____
_____
_____
_____

SECTION II: ACTIVITY HANDOUTS

Family Relationships

It is important for anyone with an addictive personality to develop and maintain positive, trusted, supportive relationships.

In the chart below, identify members of your family and describe how they support you in a healthy way, with your good and welfare in mind, or in an unhealthy way. (Use name codes.)

Family Member	Ways this Person Helps and Supports Me in a Healthy Way	Ways this Person DOES NOT Help and Support Me in a Healthy Way
Ex: MGM	He loves me unconditionally, no matter what I do.	
Ex: LBR		Her expectations of me are unrealistic and I can't live up to them.

SECTION II: ACTIVITY HANDOUTS

Friend Relationships

In the chart below, identify your friends and describe how they support you in a healthy way, with your good and welfare in mind, or in an unhealthy way.
(Use name codes.)

My Friend	Ways this Person Helps and Supports Me in a Healthy Way	Ways this Person DOES NOT Help and Support Me in a Healthy Way
Ex: GDB	She is always there for me.	
Ex: NBH		Pushes me to do things that are destructive.

SECTION II: ACTIVITY HANDOUTS

Life Skills

Developing effective life skills can help you overcome potential addictions in your life. By being able to solve problems effectively, set and work toward goals, resolving conflicts and handling stress, and developing varied interests can help you develop greater wellness and lower your dependency on specific habits.

In the spaces that follow, give yourself a grade from A to F in each of the life skill categories, and explore how you can improve your grade.

Life Skill	Grade	How I Can Improve
Solving Problems with Friends & Family		
Setting Long and Short-Term Goals for My Life		
Resolving Conflicts		
Handling Stress		
Identifying Interests		
Developing A Life Plan		
Other		

What additional life skills may be helpful for you to overcome your potential addictions?

_____
_____
_____

SECTION II: ACTIVITY HANDOUTS

Distractions

People with addictive personalities often feel the need to be distracted from everyday life in order to forget and escape from their problems. What do you do to distract yourself, which has either resulted in an addiction or is on the way to becoming an addiction? (Use Name Codes.)

Where	What Do I Do to Distract Myself?
Ex: In my personal life	When I go out with MFJ and drink alcohol, I forget my problems for a while.
In my personal life	
At school	
At my job or volunteer work	
Other	

SECTION II: ACTIVITY HANDOUTS

My Risky Distractions

1. When you are trying to distract yourself, what types of risks do you tend to take?

   _____
   _____
   _____
   _____

2. What types of risks do you feel yourself needing to take more and more often?

   _____
   _____
   _____
   _____

3. Which of these risks do you know you really should not continue to take?

   _____
   _____
   _____
   _____

4. Which of these risks do you know is foolish?

   _____
   _____
   _____
   _____

5. Which of these risks could get you in big, big trouble?

   _____
   _____
   _____
   _____

> **It is probably time to evaluate your risks
> and how these risks could affect your future.**

SECTION II: ACTIVITY HANDOUTS

"Socially Acceptable"

When most people think of addictions, they might think about illegal substances like marijuana, cocaine, and heroin. However, there are some substances that are also dangerous, but which seem more acceptable in society because they can be purchased legally, like energy drinks, tobacco, alcohol, cigarettes, and steroids.

Describe your involvement with these types of addictions.

Addiction	When and How Often?	What I Gain	What I Lose
EX: Cigarettes, Cigars, Chewing Tobacco	I smoke every chance I get.	It calms me. I feel cool. I hang out with other cool kids to smoke.	It is very expensive. I'm told I smell bad. My grandma died of lung cancer.
Cigarettes, Cigars, Chewing Tobacco			
Beer, Wine, Alcohol, Other			
Steroids			
Energy Drinks			
Other			

What changes do you want to (or should you) make in your use of the above products?

_____

_____

_____

SECTION III:
Am I Addicted? Scale

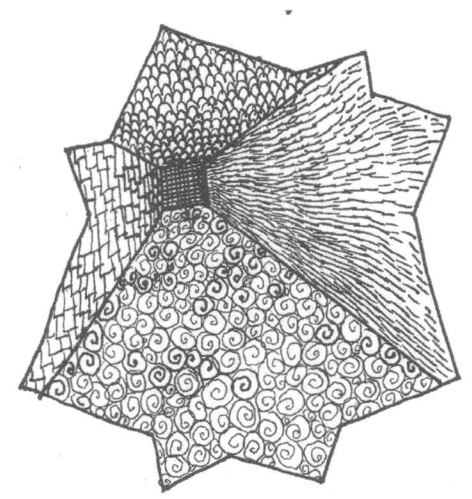

Name_____

Date_____

SECTION III: AM I ADDICTED? SCALE

Habits I Overdo (For Your Eyes Only!)

When we overdo a habit, we start relying on it. Often, that reliance becomes an addiction, regardless of how negatively it affects physical, mental, social and emotional well being or what consequences occur. The addiction then becomes extremely difficult to quit because of psychological, emotional, habitual and physical withdrawal symptoms.

Check the habits you are overdoing. Be honest! No one else needs to see this page.

- ❏ Alcohol
- ❏ Arson
- ❏ Betting
- ❏ Body building
- ❏ Bullying, sadism, masochism
- ❏ Caffeine
  (energy drinks, coffee, tea, soft drinks, chocolate)
- ❏ Card game
- ❏ Collecting unreasonably
- ❏ Crime
- ❏ Cyber sex
- ❏ Eating disorders
- ❏ Email
- ❏ Excessive fanaticizing
- ❏ Exercise too much
- ❏ Food
- ❏ Gambling
- ❏ Illegal drugs
- ❏ Internet
- ❏ Legal drugs
- ❏ Love obsessively
- ❏ Online games
- ❏ Over-sleeping
- ❏ Over-the-counter medications
- ❏ Money
- ❏ Nicotine
  (cigarettes, cigars, chewing tobacco)
- ❏ Pornography
- ❏ Prescription drugs
- ❏ Relationship neediness
- ❏ Risky behavior
- ❏ Self-injury
- ❏ Sex
- ❏ Shopping
- ❏ Shopping online
- ❏ Smoking
- ❏ Social networking sites
- ❏ Solvents (glue, aerosol sprays, gasoline)
- ❏ Sports obsession
- ❏ Stealing/shoplifting
- ❏ Steroids
- ❏ Sugar
- ❏ Texting/sexting
- ❏ Thrills
- ❏ Video games
- ❏ Workaholism
- ❏ _____
- ❏ _____
- ❏ _____
- ❏ _____

Am I Addicted?
Scale Directions

The Am I Addicted? Scale can help you determine the level and nature of your addiction.

This scale contains 36 statements. Read each of the statements and decide whether or not the statement describes you. In each of the choices listed, circle the number of your response on the line to the right of each statement.

Complete the following scale with a separate photocopy for each of the habits you checked off on the handout, *Habits I Overdo (For Your Eyes Only!)*

In the following example, the circled 4 indicates the statement is very much like the person completing the scale.

| 4 = Very Much Like Me | 3 = Usually Like Me | 2 = Somewhat Like Me | 1 = Not Like Me |

Because of this habit _____,

1. I feel bad most of the time unless I am participating in this habit ... (4)   3   2   1

This is not a test, and there are no right or wrong answers. Do not spend too much time thinking about your answers. Your initial response will likely be the most true for you. Be sure to respond to every statement.

(Turn to the next page and begin)

SECTION III: AM I ADDICTED? SCALE

Am I Addicted? Scale

4 = Very Much Like Me **3 = Usually Like Me** **2 = Somewhat Like Me** **1 = Not Like Me**

Because of this habit _____,

1. I feel bad most of the time unless I am participating in this habit 4   3   2   1
2. I have difficulty in thinking, remembering, and doing things I used to be able to do 4   3   2   1
3. People have called me names or labeled me as an addict. 4   3   2   1
4. I am having problems in school 4   3   2   1
5. Sometimes I can't remember what I have done. 4   3   2   1
6. I'm too preoccupied with this habit to make important life decisions... 4   3   2   1
7. Nothing else is as important in my life as this habit............... 4   3   2   1
8. I'm waiting for a Higher Power to save me 4   3   2   1
9. It often takes more and more of my habit to get the same effect..... 4   3   2   1
10. I often leave relationships...................................... 4   3   2   1
11. I usually feel alone and lost 4   3   2   1
12. I cannot control or quit this habit 4   3   2   1
13. I hang around other people who have the same habit 4   3   2   1
14. I often avoid spending time with family in order to participate in this habit 4   3   2   1
15. Sometimes people tell me I have a problem 4   3   2   1
16. I get pushy or show off around other people 4   3   2   1
17. I make excuses for my habit.................................... 4   3   2   1
18. I hide and sneak my addiction so people will not know.. 4   3   2   1

(Continued on the next page)

Am I Addicted? Scale *(Continued)*

4 = Very Much Like Me   **3 = Usually Like Me**   **2 = Somewhat Like Me**   **1 = Not Like Me**

Because of this habit _____,

19. I feel afraid and I am on guard all the time 4   3   2   1

20. I make promises but have trouble keeping them 4   3   2   1

21. I am desperate to get more money to afford my addiction. 4   3   2   1

22. I get into trouble because of my addiction 4   3   2   1

23. I use this habit to not feel my feelings 4   3   2   1

24. I rarely want to do anything that does not involve my addiction 4   3   2   1

25. I do things that I never thought I would do 4   3   2   1

26. I don't eat healthy foods or eat at a regular time 4   3   2   1

27. I don't care that I am less responsible than I used to be 4   3   2   1

28. I don't listen when other people try to talk with me about my addictions 4   3   2   1

29. I often hangout with people who are worse off than I am so I can feel better about myself. 4   3   2   1

30. I get the shakes, sweats, or feel anxious unless I can indulge in my habit. 4   3   2   1

31. I feel bad about how my addiction hurts other people, but I can't stop 4   3   2   1

32. I use my habit to cope with my problems. 4   3   2   1

33. My addiction is the most important thing to me right now 4   3   2   1

34. I don't care how I get money for my habit, just so I get what I need . . . 4   3   2   1

35. I do what I need to do to support my habit 4   3   2   1

36. I sometimes wonder if life just isn't worth living 4   3   2   1

(Go to the Scoring Directions on the next page)

© 2013 WHOLE PERSON ASSOCIATES, 101 W. 2ND ST., SUITE 203, DULUTH MN 55802 ▪ 800-247-6789

SECTION III: AM I ADDICTED? SCALE SCALE

Am I Addicted? Scale
Scoring Directions

The *Am I Addicted?* scale is designed to help you measure whether you are addicted and your level of addiction. Four areas have been identified to make up the scales for this assessment: Physical, Behavioral, Emotional and Psychological. The items that make up each of the four scales are grouped so that you can explore how your addictions are showing themselves.

To score your *Am I Addicted?* scale:

1. Record each of the scores from the previous two pages on the lines below. For example, if you circled the 4 for item number 1, you would put a 4 on the line above the 1 on the chart below. Do the same for all 36 items.

2. Add the totals for each of the 4 rows and put that total on the total line to the right.

___	___	___	___	___	___	___	___	___	___
1	5	9	13	17	21	25	29	33	Physical Total
2	6	10	14	18	22	26	30	34	Behavioral Total
3	7	11	15	19	23	27	31	35	Emotional Total
4	8	12	16	20	24	28	32	36	Psychological Total

GRAND TOTAL _____

The Profile Interpretation section on the next page can help you interpret your scores on the *Am I Addicted?* Scale.

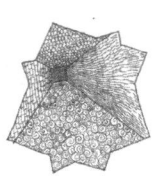

Profile Interpretation

The remainder of this scale contains interpretation materials to help determine the level and nature of your addiction. This scale can help you to identify whether your habit is an addiction and if it is, is it primarily Physical, Behavioral, Emotional, and/or Psychological in nature.

Total Score for Each of the Scales	Grand Total Score of All Four of the Scales	Result	Indications
15 to 36	56 to 144	High	You are definitely experiencing many difficulties associated with this habit which may or already be an addiction.
12 to 14	45 to 55	Moderate	You are definitely experiencing difficulties associated with this habit that may be leading to an addiction.
9 to 11	36 to 44	Low	You are probably not experiencing many of the difficulties associated with addictions, but as long as you scored any at all, you DO have a potential problem that could lead to an addiction.

Read the descriptions on the page that follows. No matter how you scored, low, moderate or high, you will benefit from the following exercises.

Am I Addicted?
Scale Descriptions

PHYSICAL – People who are addicted fail to take adequate care of themselves because they are preoccupied with their addiction. They may not sleep enough, take unnecessary risks, often skip meals and do not eat or drink healthy. They often feel bad physically and start to find themselves making excuses. They find that it often takes more and more of their addiction to feel the same effects they had been feeling, and that it may take longer to feel those effects. They find themselves starting to forget things and often find themselves doing things they never thought they would. Their addiction rapidly becomes the most important thing in their lives.

BEHAVIORAL – People who are addicted often have difficulty maintaining relationships with others, unless those others have the same addictions and encourage them in the addiction. Those peers aren't encouraging people, but many teens feel those relationships are very important. They often lose their sense of self and their connection to others. In addition, they may start to have trouble at school, work, volunteer jobs, or with family and friends. They find themselves beginning to have trouble making decisions and completing tasks. They frequently change classes, jobs and friends. They avoid friends and family who have already or may find out about their addiction. They often begin to hide, sneak and steal. They also find themselves feeling anxious.

EMOTIONAL – People who are addicted generally have low self-esteem. They tend to experience feelings such as anxiety, fear, guilt, depression and shame. They tend to have unexplained mood swings and are likely to have episodes of anger and rage. They tend to have problems and like to be distracted and consumed by their addictions, rather than discussing or working on their emotional problems. At times they will even be violent with others around them. They often feel like they are not good at anything but their addiction. They sometimes feel alone, lost and afraid. They feel angry and resentful, and then feel guilty about the effect that their addiction has on people around them.

PSYCHOLOGICAL – People addicted often experience difficulty in their thinking. They tend to have impaired reasoning and judgment. They are often unable to think things through logically. Their faulty thinking affects their performance at school, work or volunteer job. They refuse to listen to other people who are talking with them about their addiction. Because they have difficulty coping with problems while they are addicted, they use the addiction to help them cope with the stressors of their lives, rather than dealing directly with the life stressors. They often have much difficulty in reasoning and in coping with their problems and they wonder if life is worth living.

SECTION III: ACTIVITY HANDOUTS

Problems in My Life

Addictions cause a variety of physical, emotional, relationship, school and career problems.
How has your addiction caused problems for you...

with your family?
_____
_____
_____

with your girl/boy friend?
_____
_____
_____

with your friends?
_____
_____
_____

in your social life?
_____
_____
_____

at school?
_____
_____
_____

(Continued on the next page)

SECTION III: ACTIVITY HANDOUTS

Problems in My Life *(Continued)*

How has your addiction caused problems for you...

at your work?

_____
_____
_____

at your volunteer place?

_____
_____
_____

with your physical health and hygiene?

_____
_____
_____

with your mental/emotional health?

_____
_____
_____

with your need for money?

_____
_____
_____

(Continued on the next page)

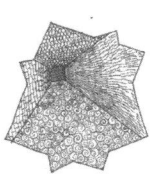

SECTION III: ACTIVITY HANDOUTS

Problems in My Life *(Continued)*

How has your addiction caused problems for you...

with the law and courts?
_____
_____
_____

with your curfews and other rules?
_____
_____
_____

with your anger and/or violent behavior?
_____
_____
_____

with your interest in favorite activities of the past?
_____
_____
_____

with anything else?
_____
_____
_____

SECTION III: ACTIVITY HANDOUTS

Self-Defeating Behaviors

A self-defeating behavior may be thoughts or behaviors that affect your motivation and personal growth, along with having a negative impact on your relationships with family or friends – with anyone!

Example: By hanging out with people who have the same behavior you are putting yourself in a situation where you will be tempted.

My self-defeating behaviors are . . .

_____
_____
_____
_____
_____
_____
_____
_____

When I am involved with my addiction I tend to . . .

_____
_____
_____
_____
_____
_____
_____
_____

When I think about myself as being addicted, I feel . . .

_____
_____
_____
_____
_____
_____
_____
_____

SECTION III: ACTIVITY HANDOUTS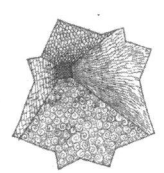

Triggers

It is also important to determine where and how you indulge in your addictions.

In the spaces that follow, for your most unhealthy addiction, identify the situations in which you find yourself indulging (or most likely to indulge), what triggers it, and who triggers it. (Use Name Codes)

My addiction is _____

Situations in Which I Indulge in my Addiction	Where or What Triggers it?	Who Triggers it?
Ex: I love sweets. Where ever someone else is having something sweet.	Just looking at anything sweet or someone talking about it . . .	My friend MLS who gets a candy bar everywhere we go.

What can you do about what or where triggers your indulgence in your addiction?
_____
_____
_____
_____

What can you do about being with the people who trigger your indulgence in your addiction?
_____
_____
_____

SECTION III: ACTIVITY HANDOUTS

Growing Up with Addiction around Me

Family history plays an important role in addictions. People are more likely to develop an addiction when they live in a family in which others are addicted.

Complete the following sentence starters to better understand addictions. (Use name codes.)

When it comes to addictions, my family at home
_____
_____
_____

When it comes to addictions, my extended family (cousins, aunts, uncles) _____
_____
_____
_____

When it comes to addictions, my family's friends and/or associates _____
_____
_____
_____

The most addictions I have seen are_____
_____
_____
_____

and by (use name codes) _____
_____
_____
_____
_____
_____

I have learned _____
_____
_____
_____from seeing others' addictions.

SECTION III: ACTIVITY HANDOUTS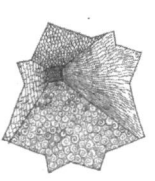

What about Me?

I like these things about myself:

_____
_____
_____
_____
_____
_____

I do not like these things about myself:

_____
_____
_____
_____
_____
_____

The ways I benefit by keeping my addiction(s).

_____
_____
_____
_____
_____
_____

The ways my addictions negatively impact my everyday life.

_____
_____
_____
_____
_____

SECTION III: ACTIVITY HANDOUTS

Non-Addicted People

People who do not have addictive thoughts, feelings and behaviors demonstrate several important traits. By answering the following questions, you will be able to explore your own addictive behaviors.

Non-Addictive People...

1) Face their problems head on.

How do you avoid or try to avoid your problems?

_____
_____
_____
_____
_____
_____
_____
_____
_____
_____

2) Recognize their limitations.

What are your limitations?

_____
_____
_____
_____
_____
_____
_____
_____
_____
_____

(Continued on the next page)

Non-Addicted People (Continued)

3) Set realistic goals.

What are your short-term goals (for the next month or so)?

_____
_____
_____
_____
_____
_____
_____
_____

What are your long-range goals (within the next six months)?

_____
_____
_____
_____
_____
_____
_____
_____

4) Appreciate their strengths.

What are your strengths?

_____
_____
_____
_____
_____
_____
_____

(Continued on the next page)

SECTION III: ACTIVITY HANDOUTS

Non-Addicted People *(Continued)*

5) Are resistant to peer pressure.

How would you describe the way you handle peer pressure?

_____
_____
_____
_____
_____
_____
_____

How would you LIKE to handle peer pressure?

_____
_____
_____
_____
_____
_____
_____

6) Are creative.

In what positive ways have you shown or expressed creativity in your life?

_____
_____
_____
_____
_____
_____

SECTION III: ACTIVITY HANDOUTS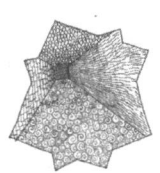

Peer Pressure

Who are the people who pressure you to be an addict? In the spaces that follow, identify those people in your life who put pressure on you. (Use name codes.)

People	Ways They Pressure Me	Why I Give In to Them

SECTION III: JOURNALING ACTIVITY

Feeling Scared?

What scares you about your addiction?

_____
_____
_____
_____
_____
_____
_____
_____
_____
_____
_____
_____
_____

What would you have to face and deal with if you gave up your addiction?

_____
_____
_____
_____
_____
_____
_____
_____
_____
_____
_____
_____

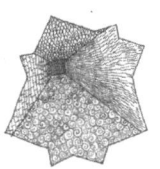

Denial that Addiction Exists

Definition: The term "denial" refers to the process by which people with addictions pretend, to themselves and/or to other people, that they do not have an addiction (when in fact they do) or that their addictive behavior is not problematic (when in fact it is). Denial may happen consciously (when people lie to cover up) or it may happen unconsciously (when they really believe that they do not have a problem.) Denial may be partially conscious (when they admit that they indulge in their addiction more than is sensible, but deny that it causes them problems) when in fact many of the problems people experience are consequences of their addiction.

People are in denial about addictions when they...

- admit they might have a problem but do not take the necessary steps to change.

- minimize the problem by saying, *"It's not so bad!"*

- blame others for their addictions.

- make excuses for themselves whenever possible.

- become angry if someone brings up the subject of any addiction, especially their own.

- distance themselves from the addiction by refusing to discuss it.

- insist that *when they are ready*, they will have no problem quitting.

- say they can stop whenever they want.

- try to quit, insist that they do not need support, a support group, and/or a professional to help them.

SECTION IV:
Am I Relapsing? Scale

Name_____

Date_____

Am I Relapsing?
Scale Directions

RELAPSE: a relapse is when a person returns to even a single incident of a substance use, activity or thoughts and behavior which had been previously discontinued.

Recovery consists of moving from the destructive effects of addictions to more healthy lifestyles and relationships. Because recovery does not happen overnight and is a developmental process that occurs over time, it is important to be vigilant about the warning signs that lead to a relapse. The *Am I Relapsing?* Scale is designed to help you identify the changes in thinking, feeling and behavior that accompany relapse.

This scale contains 39 statements that are divided into three categories: Changes in Thinking, Changes in Feelings, and Changes in Behavior. Read each of the statements and decide whether or not the statement describes you. **If the statement *does* describe you, circle the YES next to that item. If the statement *does not* describe you, circle the NO next to that item.**

In the following example, the circled Yes indicates the statement is descriptive of the person completing the scale.

Scale T

I am having trouble thinking clearly . . . . (YES)   NO

This is not a test, and there are no right or wrong answers. Do not spend too much time thinking about your answers. Your initial response will likely be the most true for you. Be sure to respond to every statement.

(Turn to the next page and begin)

SECTION IV: AM I RELAPSING? SCALE

Am I Relapsing? Scale

Scale T

I am having trouble thinking clearly.	YES	NO
I am unable to solve simple problems	YES	NO
My mind often races or wanders	YES	NO
I am having trouble concentrating.	YES	NO
I have been making bad decisions lately	YES	NO
At times I find it difficult to remember things	YES	NO
It is difficult for me to learn new information	YES	NO
I am getting confused more often and for longer periods	YES	NO
Sometimes I am not sure what is right or what is wrong.	YES	NO
I easily get frustrated and nasty.	YES	NO
I find myself losing my temper more and more.	YES	NO
Sometimes I just don't care about anything.	YES	NO
I am thinking of resuming my addiction, but not doing it as often	YES	NO

T – TOTAL = _____

(Go to the next page for Part II)

SECTION IV: AM I RELAPSING? SCALE

Am I Relapsing? Scale

Scale F

I am having trouble controlling my feelings.	**YES**	**NO**
I find myself becoming angry easily	**YES**	**NO**
I sometimes can't feel anything	**YES**	**NO**
I miss my addiction	**YES**	**NO**
I often have strong mood swings.	**YES**	**NO**
I often try to ignore or hide my feelings	**YES**	**NO**
I have been feeling sad	**YES**	**NO**
I sometimes feel a lack of control in my life.	**YES**	**NO**
I am very worried and really need a distraction	**YES**	**NO**
I have begun to feel like a failure	**YES**	**NO**
I sometimes experience periods of deep depression	**YES**	**NO**
My life often feels out of control	**YES**	**NO**
I'm feeling overwhelmed	**YES**	**NO**

F – TOTAL = _____

(Go to the next page for Part III)

SECTION IV: AM I RELAPSING? SCALE

Am I Relapsing? Scale

Scale B

I do not have the energy I used to	YES	NO
I make plans which often don't work out	YES	NO
I am having more stress out times than usual	YES	NO
I have an eating issue	YES	NO
I can't seem to get things done	YES	NO
I am having trouble sleeping regularly	YES	NO
I am not able to follow through with anything	YES	NO
My daily routine has become irregular	YES	NO
I have started missing therapy and/or support groups	YES	NO
I find myself lying to others more often	YES	NO
I can't seem to get going when I need to	YES	NO
I often do foolish things without thinking first	YES	NO
I have been spending a lot of time all alone	YES	NO

B – TOTAL = _____

(Go to the Scoring Directions on the next page)

Am I Relapsing? Scale
Scoring Directions

The *Am I Relapsing?* Scale is designed to help you determine if you are beginning to relapse into your addiction. It identifies significant changes in your thinking, feelings and behaviors. For each of the sections on the previous pages, count the number of YES answers you circled in each section. Put that number on the line marked "TOTAL" at the end of each.

Transfer your totals to the spaces below:

Scale T = Changes in Thinking Total = _____

Scale F = Changes in Feelings Total = _____

Scale B = Changes in Behavior Total = _____

Profile Interpretation

Total Individual Scale Scores	Grand Total Scales Scores	Result	Indications
Scores from 6 to 13	Scores from 16 to 39	high	You are definitely showing many signs of relapsing back into your addiction. You are experiencing major changes in your thoughts, feelings and actions.
Scores from 3 to 5	Scores from 7 to 15	moderate	You are showing signs of relapse. You are experiencing major changes in your thoughts, feelings and actions.
Scores from 0 to 2	Scores from 0 to 6	low	You tend not to be in too much danger of relapse. You do not seem to be experiencing very many major changes in your thoughts, feelings or actions. Be aware of the few signs you are showing.

The Scales in which you scored in the "Moderate" and "High" ranges tend to be warning you about the possibility of a relapse. Now go to the next section for a description of each of the three scales. Then complete the exercises that are included. No matter how you scored, low, moderate or high, you need and will benefit from these exercises.

SECTION IV: AM I RELAPSING? SCALE

Am I Relapsing?
Scale Descriptions

SCALE T

CHANGES IN THINKING includes a preoccupation with whatever you are addicted to, lack of clear thinking and poor decision-making. These types of problems in your thinking can cause you to relapse or hinder your progress in recovery. Changes in thinking can come from a variety of self-defeating thoughts. People scoring moderate or high on this scale also begin to have problems concentrating on single topics, find learning new things very difficult, become confused more easily and more often, have trouble solving problems and remembering things, and find that their thinking begins to trigger feelings of frustration and depression.

SCALE F

CHANGES IN FEELINGS includes inability to control your emotions, sudden feelings of depression and a lower self-concept. These types of problems in feelings can cause you to relapse or to hinder your progress in recovery. People scoring moderate or high on this scale also begin to feel helpless over what happens in their lives, feel like a failure, have feelings of powerlessness in their lives, over-react emotionally with others, work to hide their true feelings, experience strong mood swings, suffer from periods of deep depression, and become angry and frustrated when they are unable to control their emotions and what happens in their lives.

SCALE B

CHANGES IN BEHAVIOR includes not having the same type of energy you used to have, inability to deal effectively with stress anymore and having trouble doing small tasks. These types of problems in behavior can cause you to relapse or to hinder your progress in recovery. People scoring moderate or high on this scale also begin to have trouble sleeping regularly, do not eat healthy, have trouble following through on obligations, fail to follow through on plans, start keeping a very irregular schedule, begin to miss their therapy and/or support groups, find themselves lying more often, have trouble completing things, spend more time alone and start to act very impulsively.

The exercises that follow are designed to help you to explore the changes that are currently taking place in your thoughts, feelings and behaviors.

SECTION IV: ACTIVITY HANDOUTS

Changes in your Thinking

The following questions are designed to help you explore changes in your thinking that might be leading to a relapse:

What thoughts are you having that are worrisome to you?

_____
_____
_____
_____

In what specific way has your thinking changed recently?

_____
_____
_____
_____

How has your recent thinking affected you?

_____
_____
_____
_____

How has your recent thinking affected others in your life?

_____
_____
_____
_____

How are these thoughts setting you up for relapse?

_____
_____
_____
_____

SECTION IV: ACTIVITY HANDOUTS

Changes in your Feelings

The following questions are designed to help you explore changes in your feelings that might be leading to a relapse:

What feelings are you having that are concerning you?
_____
_____
_____
_____

In what specific way have your feelings changed recently?
_____
_____
_____
_____

How have your recent feelings affected you?
_____
_____
_____
_____

How have your recent feelings affected others in your life?
_____
_____
_____
_____

How are these feelings setting you up for relapse?
_____
_____
_____
_____

Changes in your Behavior

The following questions are designed to help you explore changes in your behavior that might be leading to a relapse:

What behaviors are you doing that are concerning you?

_____
_____
_____
_____

In what specific way has your behavior changed recently?

_____
_____
_____
_____

How has your recent behavior affected you?

_____
_____
_____
_____

How has your recent behavior affected others in your life?

_____
_____
_____
_____

How are these behaviors setting you up for relapse?

_____
_____
_____
_____

SECTION IV: ACTIVITY HANDOUTS

My History

Many people who relapse into their addiction have recurring life patterns from the past that keep them from coping well in the present. It is important to identify the life patterns that may be setting you up for a relapse. Complete the following questions about your life and your attempts to cope with life problems. When you have answered all of the My History questions, look for self-defeating patterns that keep reoccurring in your life. (Use Name Codes.)

How would you describe your family at home?

_____
_____
_____
_____
_____
_____
_____

How would you describe your relationship with your family at home?

_____
_____
_____
_____
_____
_____
_____

What negative experiences have happened?

_____
_____
_____
_____
_____
_____
_____

(Continued on the next page)

My History *(Continued)*

What types of addictions do members of your family have? (name codes)
___
___
___
___

How do these affect or influence you?
___
___
___
___
___

What types of addictions do your friends and/or peer group have?
___
___
___
___

How does this affect or influence you?
___
___
___
___

How is your addiction similar to others in your life?
___
___
___
___

SECTION IV: ACTIVITY HANDOUTS

Recovery Management

Developing and following a plan for managing your recovery is one of the most important things you can do to control your addiction and prevent relapse. Four elements of an effective plan include professional counseling, stress management, proper diet and health, and support groups.

Complete each of these four sections:

I. PROFESSIONAL COUNSELING

I am attending professional counseling.   _____Yes   _____No

The greatest benefits of attending the sessions are . . .

_____
_____
_____

The reasons I have not been attending professional counseling are . . .

_____
_____
_____

II. STRESS MANAGEMENT TECHNIQUES

I am using stress management techniques.   _____Yes   _____No

The greatest benefits of doing this are . . .

_____
_____
_____

The reasons I have not been using stress management techniques are . . .

_____
_____
_____

(Continued on the next page)

SECTION IV: ACTIVITY HANDOUTS

Recovery Management *(Continued)*

III. DIET AND HEALTH MANAGEMENT

I am living a healthy life. _____Yes _____No

How much sleep did you get last night? Was it enough or too much? Explain.

_____
_____
_____

What did you eat yesterday? Was it well balanced? Was it healthy?

_____
_____
_____

Follow your progress daily in a journal or notebook. Keep track of how much you are sleeping (naps and nights' sleep) and what you are eating.

IV. SUPPORT GROUPS or PROGRAMS

I am attending support groups or programs regularly. _____Yes _____No

List the groups and programs you have attended that you LIKE and the reasons why.

_____
_____
_____

List the groups and programs you have attended that you DO NOT LIKE and why.

_____
_____
_____

SECTION IV: ACTIVITY HANDOUTS

How Thinking Affects Potential Relapse

The way you think about an experience or problem can influence your reaction. Reframing involves presenting an alternative possible explanation, interpretation or perception of your thinking. This new interpretation can create a positive change. Complete the following table to explore the affect of your thinking on your potential relapse.

Day	Event	Your Destructive Thoughts	New Positive Thoughts
Sun.			
Mon.			
Tues.			
Wed.			
Thu.			
Fri.			
Sat.			

Photocopy and use this day after day, week after week, to track your success in reframing your destructive thoughts into positive ones.

SECTION IV: ACTIVITY HANDOUTS

How Feelings Affect Potential Relapse

The way you feel about an experience or problem can influence your reaction. Reframing involves presenting an alternative possible explanation, interpretation or perception of your feelings. This new interpretation can create a positive change. Complete the following table to explore the affect of your feelings on your potential relapse.

Day	Event	Your Negative Feelings	New Positive Feelings
Sun.			
Mon.			
Tues.			
Wed.			
Thu.			
Fri.			
Sat.			

Photocopy and use this day after day, week after week, to track your success in reframing your negative feelings into positive ones.

SECTION IV: ACTIVITY HANDOUTS

How Behaviors Affect Potential Relapse

The way you behave about an experience or problem can influence your reaction. Reframing involves presenting an alternative possible explanation, interpretation or perception of your behaviors. This new interpretation can create a positive change. Complete the following table to explore the affect of your behaviors on your potential relapse.

Day	Event	Your Negative Behaviors	New Positive Behaviors
Sun.			
Mon.			
Tues.			
Wed.			
Thu.			
Fri.			
Sat.			

Photocopy and use this day after day, week after week, to track your success in reframing your negative behaviors into positive ones.

Plan for Action to Prevent Relapse

What action will you be taking?	Who can help you? (name codes)	Why have you selected this person?	How can you reward yourself in a healthy way for taking this action?

SECTION IV: EDUCATIONAL HANDOUTS

Relapse Quotation

Jimmy Connors is a former World Number 1 tennis player from the Unites States. He said ...

> *Rather than viewing a brief relapse back to inactivity as a failure, treat it as a challenge and try to get back on track as soon as possible.*

What are some of your challenges?
_____
_____
_____
_____
_____
_____
_____
_____

What are you going to do to get back on track, and how?
_____
_____
_____
_____
_____
_____
_____
_____

When?
_____
_____

SECTION V:
Can I Stop? Scale

Name_____

Date_____

SECTION V: CAN I STOP? SCALE

Can I Stop? Scale
Directions

People may realize that they have some type of an addiction problem, but then justify it by creating alibis, making excuses or blocking out unpleasant memories or consequences of their addictive behaviors. They usually believe they have good reasons for continuing with their addiction. The *Can I Stop?* Scale is designed to get a clearer picture of the excuses that you may be using to continue your addiction, which prevents you from stopping, even though you know you should.

At the top of the scale, write the addiction for which you will be responding. If you have multiple addictions, complete one scale for each.

This scale contains statements divided into four categories. Read each of the statements and decide how descriptive the statement is of you and one of your addictions. In each of the choices listed, circle the number of your response on the line to the right of each statement.

In the following example, the circled 2 indicates the statement is a little descriptive of the person completing the inventory:

My addiction is _____

	A Lot Like Me	Somewhat Like Me	A Little Like Me	Not Like Me

I.
Because of this addiction ...

I am so calm I can't get anything done 4   3   (2)   1

This is not a test and there are no right or wrong answers. Do not spend too much time thinking about your answers. Your initial response will likely be the most true for you. Be sure to respond to every statement.

(Turn to the next page and begin)

SECTION V: CAN I STOP? SCALE

Can I Stop? Scale

My addiction is _____

I.

	A Lot Like Me	Somewhat Like Me	A Little Like Me	Not Like Me
Because of this addiction ...				
I am so calm I can't get anything done	4	3	2	1
I constantly worry about someone catching me	4	3	2	1
I get so distracted that I don't care about anything at all	4	3	2	1
I am so creative I think I can do anything, even if it's risky	4	3	2	1
I ignore my problems and do nothing about them	4	3	2	1
I stop thinking about anything that upsets me, even if I need to face an issue	4	3	2	1
I can get through the day but other times don't want to live	4	3	2	1
I say "who cares!"	4	3	2	1

I. TOTAL = _____

II.

	A Lot Like Me	Somewhat Like Me	A Little Like Me	Not Like Me
Because of this addiction ...				
I need more money	4	3	2	1
I have to work too many hours to get the money I need	4	3	2	1
My allowance/income isn't enough	4	3	2	1
I can't hold down a job	4	3	2	1
I'm taking or stealing money from wherever I can	4	3	2	1
I'm borrowing money from friends and then avoiding them	4	3	2	1
I'm making up excuses with my family to get more money from them	4	3	2	1
I am always broke	4	3	2	1

II. TOTAL = _____

(Continued on the next page)

Can I Stop? Scale *(Continued)*

III.

Because of this addiction ...

	A Lot Like Me	Somewhat Like Me	A Little Like Me	Not Like Me
I am less sad and depressed	4	3	2	1
I feel less isolated	4	3	2	1
I am more confident	4	3	2	1
I feel more grown up	4	3	2	1
I feel the courage to face life	4	3	2	1
I forget painful memories	4	3	2	1
I feel more calm	4	3	2	1
I feel more social with others who have the same addiction	4	3	2	1

III. TOTAL = _____

IV.

Because of this addiction ...

	A Lot Like Me	Somewhat Like Me	A Little Like Me	Not Like Me
I can relax	4	3	2	1
I am able to fall asleep more easily	4	3	2	1
I don't feel my aches and pains so much	4	3	2	1
Food tastes better	4	3	2	1
I have less anxiety and/or shakiness	4	3	2	1
I can talk with others easier	4	3	2	1
I feel good a lot of the time	4	3	2	1
I feel a high that I love	4	3	2	1

IV. TOTAL = _____

(Go to the Scoring Directions on the next page)

SECTION V: CAN I STOP? SCALE

Can I Stop? Scale
Scoring Directions

People who are trying to quit an addiction face many roadblocks. Four major roadblocks are Mental, Financial, Emotional and Physical. The *Can I Stop?* Scale is designed to measure which roadblocks may be keeping you from quitting, and the following pages will help to guide you through those roadblocks.

For each of the four sections on the previous pages, count the scores you circled. Put that sum on the line marked "Total" at the end of each section.

Then, transfer your totals to the spaces below:

      I. **Mental Roadblocks**   Total   = _____

     II. **Financial Roadblocks**   Total   = _____

    III. **Emotional Roadblocks**   Total   = _____

    IV. **Physical Roadblocks**   Total   = _____

Profile Interpretation

Total Individual Scales Scores	Result	Indications
Scores from 25 to 32	high	You have many roadblocks that keep you from quitting your addiction. You need to do much more to eliminate these roadblocks.
Scores from 16 to 24	moderate	You have some roadblocks keeping you from quitting your addiction. You need to do more to eliminate these roadblocks.
Scores from 8 to 15	low	You do not have too many roadblocks that keep you from quitting your addiction. It will be good to eliminate those.

For scales which you scored in the **Moderate** or **High** range, find the descriptions on the pages that follow. Then, read the description and complete the exercises that are included. No matter how you scored, low, moderate or high, you will benefit from these exercises.

Mental Roadblocks

People who experience mental roadblocks continue with their addiction because they believe it helps their mental state. When they are participating in their addiction, the world seems easier to manage. They believe that their addiction relieves a lot of their stress and they tend to worry less. They also feel as if it helps them get through the day and prevents them from being upset about things that go wrong in their lives. They believe that they are less bored and even more creative when they are involved with their addictions.

What are some negative beliefs you have about yourself?

___

What types of things do you worry about?

___

How do you believe that your addictions help you deal more effectively with your day-to-day stress?

___

(Continued on the next page)

SECTION V: ACTIVITY HANDOUTS

Mental Roadblocks (Continued)

How could you deal more effectively with your day-to-day stress without your addiction?
___
___
___
___
___

How do your addictions allow you to be more creative?
___
___
___
___
___

How could you be creative without your addiction?
(If you are creative while involved with your addiction, try doing it now. It may still work!)
___
___
___
___
___

What can you do to be prepared mentally to live a good life without your addiction?
___
___
___
___
___

Permission-Giving Thoughts for Mental Roadblocks

What permission-giving thoughts do you come up with to continue your addictions?
Look at some of the examples listed below and some of the alternative thoughts that you could be saying to yourself.

Permission-Giving Thoughts	Alternative Thoughts
1. "I can handle my cutting." 2. "Nobody will know if I have just one more joint." 3. "A drink will calm my nerves." 4. "My friends won't like me if I don't do what they do." 5. "Everyone gambles after school."	1. "I know I will need to get some help very soon." 2. "I will know!" 3. "Being anxious is better than being drunk and doing something dumb! I need to find a better way to be calm." 4. "I am not going to worry about what other people think. I'll find other friends." 5. "Just because everyone else is doing something does not mean that I have to."

You Try It

Now you try it. In the first column list your thoughts that interfere with stopping your addiction. In the second column list some of the alternative thoughts that you can substitute for your permission-giving thoughts.

Permission-Giving Thoughts	Alternative Thoughts

SECTION V: ACTIVITY HANDOUTS

Financial Roadblocks

Although it is impossible to put a dollar amount on the total cost of addiction, one thing is certain – addiction is expensive. People don't realize the true cost of addiction because it is a slow and steady drain on finances, friendships, school, careers, and eventually, life itself.

Take time to understand how addictions will impact your life.

People who are experiencing financial roadblocks continue to participate in their addictions and use any means possible. Often, they get to the point where they don't care where they get their money, who they get it from or how it affects the people from whom they are borrowing or stealing it from. They lose sight of the damage they are doing to others and ignore the fact that they can possibly be in a lot of trouble and face legal issues. These issues will become part of their records, keeping them from going to college or obtaining jobs. They may be incarcerated.

Who are your friends who have addictions? (Use name codes) How do they afford them?

_____
_____
_____
_____

How do you afford your addiction?

_____
_____
_____
_____

What kind of consequences might you have for getting money in these ways for your addictions? Would it be worth it? Why or why not?

_____
_____
_____
_____

(Continued on the next page)

Financial Roadblocks *(Continued)*

How much money did you spend last week on your addiction? List the items.
_____
_____
_____
_____

What could you have done with that money for yourself?
_____
_____
_____
_____

What could you have done with that money for your home or family?
_____
_____
_____
_____

What charity could have used that money as a donation?
_____
_____
_____
_____

What person in need could you have helped with that money?
_____
_____
_____
_____

SECTION V: ACTIVITY HANDOUTS

Emotional Roadblocks

People who are experiencing emotional roadblocks continue to be addicted because they believe that their addiction affect their emotions in positive ways. They believe they feel more confident in themselves and in their abilities. They are able to forget negative events that happened in the past, and that they face life more easily in the present. They believe their addiction helps them feel less depressed and less lonely, and that it provides them with the courage they need to face life. They also believe that they are cool and that other people accept them for who they are. They do not realize that these people accept them for their addiction.

What are your limitations? How can you overcome them without being under the influence of your addiction? (If you do not know the answer to this, speak with a counselor.)

_____
_____
_____
_____

What feelings or emotions do you express well? To whom do you express them?
(Use name codes)

_____
_____
_____
_____

Other than your addiction(s), what makes you feel good about yourself?

_____
_____
_____
_____

What can you do to have more consistent feelings about yourself?

_____
_____
_____
_____

SECTION V: ACTIVITY HANDOUTS

Physical Roadblocks

People with physical roadblocks believe their addictions help them physically. They believe that they can talk more easily to other people and fall asleep more easily at night. They believe their addiction dulls their chronic pain.

How do you keep yourself physically healthy?
_____
_____
_____
_____

What kind of exercise do you do?
_____
_____
_____
_____

What about your eating habits? How many meals per day? Protein? Fruit and vegetables? Water?
_____
_____
_____
_____

Within the next week, research if and how your addiction is harming your physical health? Write it below.
_____
_____
_____
_____

(Continued on the next page)

SECTION V: ACTIVITY HANDOUTS

Physical Roadblocks (Continued)

How does your addiction control or relieve pain for you?

_____
_____
_____
_____

Do you have any difficulty going to sleep or staying asleep? How many hours do you sleep each night?

_____
_____
_____
_____

How active is your lifestyle? Describe it. If your lifestyle is not active, why not?

_____
_____
_____
_____

What types of physical activities would you like to begin or do more of?

_____
_____
_____
_____

(Continued on the next page)

SECTION V: ACTIVITY HANDOUTS

Physical Roadblocks (Continued)

What can you do to increase your physical wellness without your addiction?
_____
_____
_____
_____

In what ways does your addiction make you feel worse physically?
_____
_____
_____
_____

In what situations do you tend to indulge in with your addiction? What triggers it?
_____
_____
_____
_____

What else could you do in those situations other than indulging in your addiction?
_____
_____
_____
_____

If you don't know the answer to the question above, who are some trusted adults you can confide in?

_____   _____
_____   _____
_____   _____
_____   _____

SECTION V: ACTIVITY HANDOUTS

Peer Pressure

Teens often are unable to stop their addictions because they are concerned about what their peers or others will do or say. In the spaces below, list the family members, friends or acquaintances who pressure you into continuing your use of the substance, identify your addiction and why you can't say no.

Addiction	Person Who Applies Pressure (use name codes)	Why I Have a Problem Saying "NO!"
Smoking	EX: MPG	It's the only way I can connect with her and she's in the popular crowd I want to be in.

What can you begin to do to be more assertive and not give way to pressure?

_____

_____

Who can help you to re-evaluate friendships and make decisions as to whether they are worth it or not?

_____

_____

SECTION V: ACTIVITY HANDOUTS

I Can Stop!

Many teens believe that it is okay to have an addiction because they believe they can quit any time they choose. They think they can do a little just for fun, to feel grown-up, for social friendship and inclusion, or for higher self-esteem. They also believe they are just doing these things "recreationally" and that they are not addicted.

However, it is not that easy to stop.

In the spaces below, identify all the ways that you rationalize your addiction(s) and why you think you can stop anytime you want to.

I think I can stop _____ because _____
_____
_____
_____

I think I can stop _____ because _____
_____
_____
_____

I think I can stop _____ because _____
_____
_____
_____

I think I can stop _____ because _____
_____
_____
_____

Do you really believe these reasons are true? _____

If so, what's stopping you from stopping? _____
_____
_____

Stages of Addiction

Stage I: Internal Change

- Person experiences the high produced by certain objects or events.
- Person experiences mood changes.
- Addictive personality settles in place.

Stage II: Lifestyle Change

- Addictive behavior begins.
- Behavioral dependency begins to develop.
- Life and relationships are arranged and guided by addictive logic.

Stage III: Life Breakdown

- Addictive personality is now in total control of person.
- Life begins to break down.
- Coping and interactions with others is difficult and filled with stress.
- Life becomes …
    - ○ expensive
    - ○ secretive
    - ○ sneaky
    - ○ resentful
    - ○ aggressive
    - ○ overwhelming
    - ○ sleepless
    - ○ depressing
    - ○ anxious
    - ○ lethargic
    - ○ filled with mood swings and reactive behavior

Which stage of addictions are you in?

SECTION VI:
Change & Recovery Scale

Name_____

Date_____

SECTION VI: CHANGE & RECOVERY SCALE

Change & Recovery Scale Directions

When you have decided that it is time to overcome your addictions, you will need a degree of self-discipline and will power.

This scale contains 15 statements related to your self-discipline and will power.
Read each of the statements and decide whether or not the statement describes you. If the statement does describe you, circle the number in the YES column next to that item. If the statement does not describe you, circle the number in the NO column next to that item.

In the following example, the circled number under YES indicates the statement is descriptive of the person completing the inventory.

My Primary Addiction is _____ *gambling* _____

		YES	NO
1.	I believe I am able to control destructive impulses	(2)	1

This is not a test and there are no right or wrong answers. Do not spend too much time thinking about your answers. Your initial response will likely be the most true for you.
Be sure to respond to every statement.

(Turn to the next page and begin)

SECTION VI: CHANGE & RECOVERY SCALE

Change & Recovery Scale

My Primary Addiction is _____

		YES	NO
1.	I believe I am able to control destructive impulses	2	1
2.	I don't have the will power to refuse to indulge in my addiction	1	2
3.	I have tremendous inner strength	2	1
4.	I can't live well without my addiction.	1	2
5.	I can reject the immediate satisfaction of my addiction for long-term gains	2	1
6.	I want to control my addiction	2	1
7.	If I decide to stop engaging in my addiction, I can stop it forever	1	2
8.	I can say "No" to my addiction	2	1
9.	I can't tell people "No"	1	2
10.	I will not give in to my addiction(s)	2	1
11.	I am able to outlast my urge to indulge in my addiction	2	1
12.	I could stop but I give into peer-pressure	1	2
13.	I have what it takes to let go of my addiction	2	1
14.	I don't need my addiction	2	1
15.	I give in easily to temptation	1	2

TOTAL = _____

(Go to the Scoring Directions on the next page)

SECTION VI: CHANGE & RECOVERY SCALE

Change & Recovery Scale
Scoring Directions

It is important to determine the level of your self-discipline and will power in combating your addictions. Add the numbers you circled on the assessment and put that total in the blank space below.

Self-Discipline & Will Power = _____

Profile Interpretation

Total Scales Scores	Result	Indications
Scores from 29 to 30	high	You tend to have great will power and self-discipline.
Scores from 26 to 28	moderate	You tend to have some will power and self-discipline, but there is room for you to improve.
Scores from 15 to 25	low	You tend to have limited will power and self-discipline. You need to do as much as possible to enhance your will power for personal and professional growth.

Regardless of how you scored on each of the scales, you will benefit from the following exercises.

SECTION VI: ACTIVITY HANDOUTS

Overcoming Addictions

Habits make life much easier! When you do the same things over and over, you don't need to think or find new ways of doing things. Soon your habits can turn into addictions, which become normal behavior for you. When your habits turn into addictions you cannot stop them even if they are problematic in your life. To break these addictions, you need to want to change, take responsibility for changing, have clear goals, and understand how you can find interests in your life other than your addiction.

Goals for Change

Being confident that you can change is critical in breaking a habit or addiction.

My addiction(s) are _____

_____

_____

_____

What do I want to change? _____

_____

_____

_____

_____

_____

How will this help me in a positive way? _____

_____

_____

_____

_____

_____

_____

My goals 1. _____   4. _____

2. _____   5. _____

3. _____   6. _____

SECTION VI: ACTIVITY HANDOUTS

Self-Worth and Self-Esteem

Teens who have addictions have a low assessment of self-worth and low self-esteem. Self-worth and self-esteem refer to how you think or feel about yourself and these feelings are reflected in all aspects of your life. When teenagers are active in their addictions, they often do not feel good about themselves. They have low self-worth and low self-esteem.

Complete the following statements to explore your self-worth.

I often reject compliments or praise because _____
_____
_____
_____
_____
_____

I often think I am not quite good enough because _____
_____
_____
_____
_____
_____

I feel different from the rest of the world because_____
_____
_____
_____
_____
_____

I am afraid to make mistakes because_____
_____
_____
_____
_____

(Continued on the next page)

Self-Worth and Self-Esteem *(Continued)*

I feel ashamed of who I am because _____

_____

_____

_____

_____

I blame myself for everything that happens because _____

_____

_____

_____

_____

Some names I have been called are _____

_____

_____

_____

_____

I wish other people would like me because _____

_____

_____

_____

_____

I feel frustrated when others do not change because _____

_____

_____

_____

_____

SECTION VI: ACTIVITY HANDOUTS

Life is Very Interesting...

> *Life is very interesting ... in the end, some of your greatest pains, become your greatest strengths.*
>
> ~ Drew Barrymore
> Quote for overcoming addiction

People with addictive personalities often become obsessed with high-risk activities because they have not yet found their true strengths, interests or passions.

1. What are you interested in pursuing or learning more about?

   _____
   _____
   _____
   _____

2. What do you want to accomplish before you are 20 years old?

   _____
   _____
   _____
   _____

3. What have you always dreamed of doing?

   _____
   _____
   _____
   _____

4. Other than an addiction, what is your burning desire in life?

   _____
   _____
   _____
   _____

(Continued on next page)

Life is Very Interesting... (Continued)

5. Other than an addiction, what were you born to do?

6. What work, or types of work, would make your life meaningful?

7. What volunteer job would make your life more meaningful?

8. What charity or cause would you like to advocate?

9. What do you love doing so much that you would do it as a volunteer?

10. What do you value most in your life?

(Continued on next page)

Life is Very Interesting... *(Continued)*

11. What have you always wanted to do, but were afraid to try?

    _____
    _____
    _____
    _____

12. If you won the lottery, what would you do with your time?

    _____
    _____
    _____
    _____

13. If you won the lottery, what would you do with your money?

    _____
    _____
    _____
    _____

14. If you won the lottery, where would you live and why?

    _____
    _____
    _____
    _____

15. Even without winning the lottery, can you see yourself doing any of these things some day? How?

    _____
    _____
    _____
    _____

SECTION VI: ACTIVITY HANDOUTS

Alternatives to Your Addictions

Once you quit your addiction, you will have a great opportunity to learn new and different things. The more alternatives you have, the healthier you will become. From the lists that follow, circle any alternatives that interest you.

CREATIVE	PHYSICAL	NATURE, etc.	SPORTS	ENTERTAINMENT
drawing	running	pets	play:	video games
writing	swimming	walking dogs	_____	theater
photography	dancing	gardening	_____	movies
making music	exercising	flowers	_____	concerts
scrapbooking	martial arts	hiking	_____	board games
crafts	canoeing	climbing	watch:	_____
_____	skiing	_____	_____	_____
_____	_____	_____	_____	_____
_____	_____	_____	_____	_____

List at least ten individual activities you will consider and how you can go about becoming involved.

_____   _____
_____   _____
_____   _____
_____   _____
_____   _____
_____   _____
_____   _____
_____   _____
_____   _____
_____   _____

Benefits of Recovery

(List a benefit of recovery that you can envision as it pertains to your life after each letter of the alphabet.)

Example: X = eXtraordinary accomplishment

A _____

B _____

C _____

D _____

E _____

F _____

G _____

H _____

I _____

J _____

K _____

L _____

M _____

N _____

O _____

P _____

Q _____

R _____

S _____

T _____

U _____

V _____

W _____

X _____

Y _____

Z _____

SECTION VI: ACTIVITY HANDOUTS

Benefits of Recovery – Examples

A Ability to cope better

B Better sleep

C Control over thoughts

D Decreased guilt

E Emotional well-being

F Freedom

G Good decision-making

H Healthy living habits

I Increased courage

J Joyful in the knowledge that I can mend some relationships

K Knowing what I need to do

L Less anxious

M Mental well-being

N Now I can control my actions

O Open to new healthy interests

P Physical well-being

Q Quality of life

R Respect of myself and others to whom I have lied

S Self-Acceptance

T Trust in myself

U Understanding what I must do to stay recovered

V Very peace-filled

W Worthy

X eXtraordinary feelings about my accomplishment

Y Yesterday was yesterday, and now a new life

Z Zealous in my determination not to relapse

SECTION VI: QUOTATIONS

Quotation: **Change**

> *Things do not change; we change.*
> ~ Henry David Thoreau

How have you changed since you began your addiction? _____
_____
_____
_____

How have your changes affected you? _____
_____
_____

How have they affected your relationships with your family? _____
_____
_____

How have they affected your relationships with your friends? _____
_____
_____

What would you like to change about your life? _____
_____
_____

How can you go about it? _____
_____
_____

If you don't know how to go about it, talk with a trusted adult or your counselor or a teacher.
_____
_____

We, the authors of this book, believe you can change if you want to! *Ester & John*

SECTION VI: QUOTATIONS

Quotation: Work in Progress

> *I am a work in progress.*
> ~ Violet Yates

What does this quote mean to you?

_____
_____
_____
_____
_____
_____
_____
_____

When it comes to you, how are you a work in progress?

_____
_____
_____
_____
_____
_____
_____
_____

What do you need to do to make progress overcoming your addictions?

_____
_____
_____
_____
_____
_____
_____
_____

SECTION VI: QUOTATIONS

Quotation: **Control**

> *You have no control over what the other person does.*
> *You only have control over what you do.*
> ~ A. J. Kitt

What does this quote mean to you?
_____
_____
_____

How do you try to control others?
_____
_____
_____

How do others try to control you?
_____
_____
_____

How does your addiction control you?
_____
_____
_____

How do you control your addiction?
_____
_____
_____

SECTION VI: QUOTATIONS

Quotation: Feeling Feelings

> *She goes from one addiction to another.*
> *All are ways for her to not feel her feelings.*
> ~ Ellen Burstyn

How can you relate to the above situation?

_____
_____
_____
_____
_____
_____
_____

Write about a time you went from one addiction to another.

_____
_____
_____
_____
_____
_____
_____

In what ways do you believe you tend to be addicted to avoid feeling your feelings? Write about this.

_____
_____
_____
_____
_____
_____
_____

SECTION VI: QUOTATIONS

Quotation: Understanding Addictions

> *It is hard to understand addiction unless you have experienced it.*
> ~ Ken Hensley

Who do you know who has overcome an addiction? What was this person's addiction?
_____
_____
_____
_____

How did this person overcome it?
_____
_____
_____
_____

Who can you talk with who has had an addiction and has overcome it? Why this person?
_____
_____
_____
_____

If you don't know of someone, speak with a school counselor or another mental health professional. Make a list below of trusted people you can ask for names of counselors or therapists, even if you need to tell them you are just asking for a friend who needs help.
_____
_____
_____
_____

SECTION VI: QUOTATIONS

Quotation: **Consequences**

> *I've seen firsthand the terrible consequences of drug abuse. My heart is with all who suffer from addiction and the terrible consequences for their families.*
>
> ~ Columba Bush

What have been your consequences of your addictions?

_____
_____
_____
_____
_____
_____

How has your addiction impacted your family?

_____
_____
_____
_____
_____
_____

How has your addiction impacted the relationships you have with your family members?

_____
_____
_____
_____
_____
_____

SECTION VI: QUOTATIONS

Quotation: **A Wish**

> *You are never given a wish without also being given the power to make it true. You may have to work for it, however.*
> ~ Richard Bach

What is one of your wishes about recovering from your addiction? _____
_____
_____
_____

To whom can you go to ask for professional help or for referrals of professional help? _____
_____
_____
_____

What are you willing to do to 'work for it'? _____
_____
_____
_____

Who can be your support system: people you can trust, people who can be cheerleaders for you and help you get through a difficult time while you 'work for it'? _____
_____
_____
_____

Please sign this page, saying you are ready to 'work for it' to stop your addiction.

_____   _____
              NAME   DATE

SECTION VI: QUOTATIONS

Serenity Prayer

(Fill in your responses on the blank lines.

Grant me the serenity

to accept the things I cannot change;

_____
_____
_____
_____
_____

courage to change the things I can;

_____
_____
_____
_____
_____

and wisdom to know the difference.

Whole Person Associates is the leading publisher of training resources for professionals who empower people to create and maintain healthy lifestyles. Our creative resources will help you work effectively with your clients in the areas of stress management, wellness promotion, mental health and life skills.

Please visit us at our web site: **www.wholeperson.com**. You can check out our entire line of products, place an order, request our print catalog, and sign up for our monthly special notifications.

Whole Person Associates

800-247-6789